Pyramid Life Center
A Writer's Memoir

by Sue Cummings

Copyright © 2022 Sue Cummings

All rights reserved.

ISBN:979-8-8477-0892-0

DEDICATION

In loving memory of Sister Monica Murphy
(1942-2019)

Pyramid Lake

View from the Boathouse

Rainbow-Colored Kayaks and Swim Float

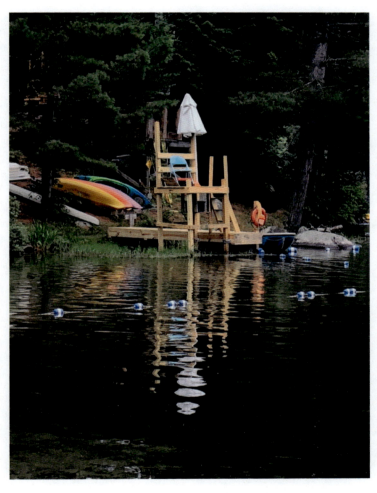

Tracy's Life Guard Stand
and
Home of the Paleozoic Immensity

The Time of Fishing

Breakfast in the Gazebo

Lakeside Path

CONTENTS

Acknowledgments   i

1   The Beginning of the Beginning   5

2   Gaining Momentum   21

3   Dancing with Audre Lorde   38

4   Rest   51

5   The End of the Beginning   64

6   Afterword   83

Morning Light in Cabin 4

ACKNOWLEDGMENTS

I wish to acknowledge my Pyramid Life Center
Women Writers' Retreat Instructors

Cynthia Brackett-Vincent, Jil Hanifan, Lalita Noronha,
Miriam Russell, Carmine Coco-DeYoung, Nan Payne,
Sandi Dollinger, Sr. Fran Dempsey, and Joanne
Van Genderen

And express my gratitude, love, and deep respect
for all the women who come together each July to
create and recreate

**The Pyramid Life Center
Women Writers' Retreat**

Feeding Time in the Loon Nursery

Pyramid Life Center

A Writer's Memoir

by Sue Cummings

Preface

Pyramid Life Center (PLC) is an Adirondack summer camp, with a lodge, dining hall, spacious log cabin chapel, boathouse and many small two-story cabins dotting the hillsides above the clean, clear water of Pyramid Lake. It is located in Paradox, New York, and sits on 750 acres of mountainous Adirondack Wilderness owned by the Diocese of Albany. From 1988-2019 its director was Sister of St. Joseph, Monica Murphy. For more than 25 years, it has been the site of the Annual-July-Pyramid Life Center-Women Writers' Retreat. It is of this retreat I write.

CHAPTER 1

THE BEGINNING OF THE BEGINNING

JULY 17ᵀᴴ – JULY 24ᵀᴴ
2015

"Why, sometimes I've believed as many as six impossible things before breakfast."

Lewis Carroll, *Alice's Adventures in Wonderland*

I came as a stranger, drenched in apprehension. I was weary too. I'd driven seven hours north to Paradox, New York, and my GPS had berated me mercilessly the last few miles as I groped for the entrance to the camp off Route 74.

*****

The road into the camp was unpaved, long, winding and narrow. There was a bridge over a stream, and at least one warning sign about honking before rounding a blind curve. The tall forest rose up around me, and the sky disappeared. Sunlight arrived in shafts, falling on rocks and ferns. An entire primeval world unfolded like a pop-up page in a children's book. It was a book my child's eye seemed to remember, and my naturalist self was eager to explore.

When the sky reappeared over the forest clearing which marked the outer edge of the camp, it was almost 4 PM. The parking lot below the dining hall was full. I turned my car around, and pulled up onto the steep, sloping shoulder of the road. I sat in my tilted car wondering if I'd made a mistake.

I'd never been to a writer's retreat. I wasn't a writer. I was a retired woman who'd taken a freshmen creative writing class at her local university in the spring, and had written a few poems. What I really was — was a *wannabe* writer — an exhausted fool, too tired to turn around and drive home.

I dragged myself out of the car, climbed the short steep hill toward the dining hall, and got my first look at Pyramid Lake. It wasn't more than a quick glance, but it was enough to let me know I could really like it here. My eyes checked out a small bathing beach, a rack of rainbow-colored kayaks, and four aluminum rowboats floating lazily alongside a nearby dock. I made a mental note, *if worse comes to worse, I can always spend my time fishing.* I'd brought my gear.

The spring on the screen door opening into the large dining hall made a sound which immediately brought me back to my childhood days at summer camp, and so did the firm snap of the door as it closed behind me. Inside the dining hall I heard another sound, one I would come to love. It was the screeching, raucous cacophony of women writer's voices greeting one another after a year-long separation.

Neil, the lanky, dark-haired, bespectacled, resident college student greeter-in-chief, checked me in and explained that *'the boys'* with the golf-cart would help me get my stuff from the car out to Cabin 4. For your edification, should you ever visit PLC, I offer here the report that Room D on the second floor of Cabin 4 is a newcomer's worst nightmare.

First of all, it's upstairs in a cabin which itself is upstairs. We're talking nose bleed elevations from the lakeside path below. Room D is a large dormitory with too many cots, and a single overhead light dangling from the ceiling. That day it was stiflingly hot, not a window open.

It was the mouse who startled me on the landing as I dragged my luggage up the narrow, dimly lit staircase, that broke me. Neil got the worst of my first-class temper, when like a rich foreign dignitary I insisted on being assigned the room with two beds, upstairs in Cabin 4 with Maddy Spadola.

Maddy was standing next to me when I planted my flag and pronounced my declaration of independence from whatever rule of law existed in terms of room assignments. Now you have to understand, I knew no one at the camp, and barely knew Maddy. I was a flat-footed *newbie*.

Maddy and I had met in early May that year at a Pema Chodron retreat in Rhinebeck, New York. I'm a long-time follower of Pema Chodron, the first ever American woman to be ordained a Tibetan Buddhist nun. I'd gifted myself the rather expensive retreat that May to celebrate my 70th birthday, and recover from the shock of the discovery of my own mortality. The previous November I'd had a double mastectomy, and I was still adjusting to the idea of death, and living with no breasts.

If you believe in chance, or synchronicity or whatever (and I do), that's how Maddy and I met. In less than twenty-four hours we'd discovered we both loved poet Billy Collins, were intensely interested in creative writing, were nearly the same age, and then Maddy thought to say the magic words… *"wouldn't it be wonderful if you came to the PLC Women Writers' Retreat in July?"*

Before I move on from my rocky beginnings at PLC, I want you to know that the next July, and the three Julys thereafter, I would take on as a privilege a willingness to be moved anywhere in the camp to accommodate a newcomer blowing a fuse. Neil and I would make move-in-day miracles happen, and many a disgruntled first-timer reaped the benefit of our arrangement.

After my own first experience, I never really cared where I landed. I was just glad to be there.

*****

My enlightenment about the value of PLC had its beginning that first night, when in a heavy soaking rain, Maddy and I with headlamps aglow were returning to Cabin 4 from our Friday evening pre-retreat poetry class with Cynthia Bracket-Vincent. It was the raindrops on the upturned leaves which caught my eye. Everywhere around us they were reflecting our light. That night I wrote in my journal... *the leaves upturned, with rain on their backs, shining like diamonds, were worth the entire day!*

The next morning I learned Neil was much more than a competent greeter-in-chief, he was a damned genius: a deadpan, straight-faced comedian, and a walking encyclopedia of *whatever you wanna know,* and what I wanted to know is where I could store my worms.

I had come to PLC to write, but also to fish. I was in a mania of fishing fever that summer. When I retired in August 2012, I'd had just one thing on my bucket list — Fly Fishing. I arrived at PLC with my New York State fishing license, and spent many hours in heaven, hiding out in a rowboat, hovering over rocks and fallen trees in a little cove, catching Blue Gill and Pumpkin Seed at will, pondering my right relationship with this intriguing assortment of women who called themselves writers. I was happy — happy to be alive, and happy to be near writers. It was a start.

Besides getting a good night's sleep, which I never did because my mind was always racing and writing, the cot and heat and sleeping bag were too much a challenge, Maddy's good company and conversation too good to miss, and of course, the forest — the forest around me was full of sights, sounds, smells, wonders beyond words and I didn't want to miss a thing — my greatest challenge was the dining hall routine. Except for Maddy, I didn't know a soul, and it was clear from how the tables filled there were deep friendships among the veterans. Armed with my own purpose for being there (I wanted to become a writer), I'd make myself walk up to a table with an empty seat and politely ask if the seat was taken. Sometimes it was, and that made me gun-shy.

I spoke with Maddy about my growing dining hall angst. She understood, and admitted she shared it. That was the break-through. Maddy and I made a pact that in the dining hall, no matter who we were with we would welcome the other. This was a psychological trick that worked out well for both of us. It wasn't long before meal time became one of the most important, enjoyable, and edifying times of my day. I never tired of the conversations going on at those tables: writers speaking with writers about writing.

Sr. Monica Murphy, Sarah (student summer worker *aka* one of Sr. Monica's *'boys'*, **Mary Pat Kane** (Women Writers' Retreat Participant), and **Neil Bradt,** my *Super-Hero-Greeter-In-Chief,* enjoying a moment of relaxed mid-afternoon conversation in the Dining Hall.

2016

On Sunday morning, I'd dawdled getting out of the dining hall, and was rushing from Cabin 4 to get to Cynthia's poetry class on time. I took a short cut to the lodge, a narrow descending, mostly untraveled footpath, and that's where I met God.

I'd seen him the evening before at Mass. He'd spoken the gospel and delivered the homily in the character and voice of Jesus. He was very convincing, so when we passed one another, I couldn't resist, and called out — *"God, I never expected to meet you in the flesh."*

He brightened and looked amused, took my lead, and replied *in character*. This led to a lengthy conversation in which I got to think about, and ask the actual questions I would ask God if I met him/her/they or whatever in the flesh. I'd tell you the questions I asked, but honestly, I don't remember them. What I do remember is this: *God was angry*, said he was *"disappointed in people, and might move to Mexico."*

Not much real-world news arrives at PLC in July. Internet and cell phone service are sparse in this area of the Adirondacks, and more or less absent when one exits the Northway onto Route 74 at Severance, New York. This fact, never ceases to amuse me, especially when I consider my destination is a place called Paradox.

That Sunday morning, however, news that Donald Trump had announced his candidacy for President in New York City had seeped through, and God was worried. He told me he lived in a small town in Maine, a place not welcoming of homosexuals, and he'd just "*come out.*" He believed Trump's candidacy and presidency would endanger him. I asked, "Why don't you make things better? Make them the way you want them? After all, *you're God!*" He told me "it didn't work that way."

I tried to comfort him. Told him I was glad to have met "God *in the flesh*," and said, more for myself to hear, "You know, we'll never be together like this again." I wondered if he might join me for lunch, and suggested we meet in the dining hall after my class.

I arrived a half-hour late to Cynthia's class, and interrupted everything. Cynthia and my classmates had worried about me. I told everyone, as succinctly as I could, that I'd met God on the path coming to class. I asked them if they wanted to know what he'd said. They indulged me, and I told them, "*he worries, just like us.*"

Cynthia Brackett-Vincent, Enjoying Some Kayak Time!
Weekend Poets of Pyramid

(Photograph Courtesy of Diane Kavanaugh-Black)

*****

On Monday morning at 9 AM, I began my first Women Writers' Retreat class with poet Jil Hanifan, who as I write this in 2022, is the Director of the State University of New York, Albany Writing Center. I say this, not to impress you, but to tell you that the writing instruction at the PLC Women Writers' Retreat is serious, and the women who attend these classes are serious about writing.

To say Jil Hanifan was a force in my life as a writer is an understatement. She's a poet's poet, and snapped me to *writerly* attention like nobody else in the world will likely ever do again. Her class was held in the largest, most spacious building, the Chapel atop a steep rocky rise over-looking the lake.

When Maddy and I entered the Chapel, there were already twenty or more women seated in a large U-shape arrangement of church pews. Jil was seated on a table, which also served as an altar for Sunday Mass, situated at the open end of the wide U. She was swinging her legs and wearing an Irish flat cap over her short-clipped hair, brim to the rear. She was a presence, and it was immediately clear *something* was going to happen here.

This is what I recall of that first class.

Jil opened with a statement as if she were setting down a marker. I can't tell you her exact words, but the meaning was this. We were here to write poetry, which meant that the emotions our writing might stir in us were not the point. The point was — the perfection of the choice and sequence, sound and rhythm, meaning and imagery of the words we wrote. Words carefully chosen and arranged to convey and awaken recognition of *an ineffable, sublimely human experience in a reader or listener.*

It was clear this was no game Jil was playing. She was dead serious about poetry, and told us she wasn't here to coddle us. I wasn't sure what this speech was intended to evoke in me, terror perhaps? Well, terror it did, but it also thrilled me.

Next, Jil asked us to answer the question: "*What Color is the Sky?*" Only she didn't want a "*correct answer,*" she wanted the "*wrongest answer!*" Oh, now *that* was an experience!

Yikes! — *which sky?* my scientist-self reflexively demanded to know, while the 17-year-old sitting next to me called out the color "*white!*" Jil answered the question with the number "22." That's the moment I felt my heart skip a beat, and my poet's life begin.

Of course, I thought — the world is full of wrong answers! I believed I understood what Jil was illustrating with her question. Poetry was *an invitation, to free ourselves* from our ordinary, habitual and conventional ways of thinking. I felt like I'd just received the best ever "*get- out- of- jail free card.*"

Each of the following nights I sat on the floor in the weak light of the upstairs hallway of Cabin 4, my notes and papers spread around me, struggling to comprehend what Jil meant when she directed us to "*use the spine*" of a Joy Harjo poem to write our own.

At the end of the week, I had two poems *after* Joy Harjo, and imagined, perhaps erroneously, Jil had found something of worth in them. On the ride home I was high as a kite, and couldn't go a mile south without pulling over to scribble. A poem was composing itself in my head. It was *The Wrongest Answer*, my first published poem, and an homage to Jil Hanifan.

the wrongest answer

when our poetics instructor asks, "what color is the sky?"
and directs us to provide the *"wrongest answer,"*
i do my best to reply.

i keep calling out, "which sky? which sky? which sky?"
my left brain rumbling along like a freight train
on a high prairie.

the nineteen-year-old poet savant sitting to my left
offers the word "white." the instructor nods approvingly,
and ends the inquiry abruptly.

"22" she states.

my brain train screeches to a halt.
billions of molecules, once in forward motion collide.
it's a cosmic pile up.

yes, 22! of course, 22! why not 22?

or 13 for that matter, or garbage pail, or god
there are so many wrong answers.
if this is poetry, i'm in! i can do this!

i float through the day supercharged on a cloud
of possibility, but at night, alone again in darkness,
i wonder a new question.

is a wrong *"wrongest"* answer more right, than a right *"wrongest"*
answer?

i worry the matter round and round, til' i slip downward
into the labyrinth, of a would-be-poet's midsummer night's
dream.

In the truth of Jil's no-nonsense speaking in 2015, I found the courage to admit that my competence as an awake and powerful human being resides entirely with my effort and desire to write. I came away from camp understanding I *was* a writer: not because I'd written anything in particular, or anything at all, but because of the way I lived my life, the way I looked out on the world. It seems I'd always been a poet, I just didn't know it. (*Does that rhyme?!*)

Giddy Up!

This is me riding *Sea Biscuit* to victory after completing Jil Hanifan's Poetry Class in 2015

Maddy Spadola, Writing on the Porch Outside Cabin 5

2019

CHAPTER 2

GAINING MOMENTUM

JULY 22ND - JULY 29TH
2016

"Second star to the right and straight on 'til morning..."

J.M. Barrie, Peter Pan

Armed with experience, I approached the 2016 PLC Women Writers' Retreat with enthusiasm. I'd brought Kim Trotto, a New Jersey writer friend with me. I was convinced every woman writer would benefit from a trip to PLC. I'd become evangelical.

Kim and I turned right off Route 74 into the camp a little after 4 PM Friday afternoon. The forest rose up around us, wickedly, eternally primeval as ever, and I was beside myself with joy, sharing this vision with Kim. When we came into the clearing that was the parking lot for the camp there was all sorts of activity: people unloading kayaks from roof racks, lugging sleeping bags and back packs up the hill to the dining hall, and the golf cart was zooming around here and there.

Several weekend only groups were arriving: an *AL- Anon* contingent, Marnie Gillard's *Weekend Storytellers*, and Cynthia Brackett-Vincent's *Weekend Poets of Pyramid*. There were many familiar faces – women like myself who had discovered how to turn the Sunday to Friday Women Writers' Retreat into seven days at PLC by adding a pre-weekend poetry or story-telling class.

Kim and I were assigned a gigantic room on the first floor of Cabin 3. I was shocked to see the size of the space, and only two beds, but the real mind blower was the two small closet sized bathrooms. It was the *Ritz*! I loved it, but Kim wasn't happy. She was unsteady on her feet on the rough terrain around the camp, and challenged by the long steep climb up the dusty road to Cabin 3. As always, Neil was a gentleman, and said Kim could move into a single room in the Lodge on Sunday before the start of the Women Writers' Retreat. Until then he'd have *'the boys'* drive her back and forth to Cabin 3 in the golf cart.

After supper, Kim set out for Marnie's Storytelling class in the Boathouse, and I climbed the steps on the grassy hill, the short-cut to Marian Lodge. I was eager to be with Cynthia Brackett-Vincent again, and the Weekend Poets of Pyramid I'd met in 2015.

Cynthia's poetry class will always be, for me, the perfect way to begin a week of writing at PLC. First of all, it's held in the Fireplace Room, which is large and has the most comfortable seating at the camp. There's an enormous comfy sectional couch, that can seat 10-15 people in a semi-circle, and with a few assorted comfortable chairs pulled into the crevices, there's luxury seating for twenty or more. The couch and chairs face a large river-rock stone fireplace, and Cynthia sits facing us with a low rectangular coffee table in front of her stacked high with handouts, books and surprises.

In this arrangement, Cynthia appears a Buddha-like figure seated in the center of the top of our semi-circle, with a perfect almost shaved head, comfortable camper's clothing, a welcoming smile, soft voice and cheerful eye. After introductions and greetings, she begins her class reading the best haiku by the greatest Haiku Masters, offering comments and instruction while she reads. I tell you, listening to Cynthia read poetry, especially haiku, is like having jasmine perfume sprayed into the air.

When the evening was over at 9:30 PM, we all floated out of the room pleasantly exhausted by our day's travel and eager to have our souls awakened in haiku surprise by the natural beauty around us. The first assignment, of course: write a haiku.

*****

That night I couldn't fall asleep, and left Kim in our luxurious space, to sit in the small dark living room which divides the first floor of Cabin 3. I took out my pen, laid my flashlight on the cushion beside me, and struggled to find a haiku worthy of the tradition. It took many false starts, but I knew I had one when I noticed the tip of my pen lit in the beam of my flashlight.

writing in the dark

tip of pen catches flash of light

pyramid magic

*****

While I was still writing, a woman entered the back door of the cabin. It was after midnight. She was having quite a time lugging herself and her stuff up the three steep back steps. I got up to give her a hand, and we whispered introductions. I explained that the room to the right was empty. I don't remember this woman's name, but I'll never forget what she shared with me. It shook me to the bones.

She explained she'd been on her way to Pyramid Life Center travelling Route 22, and had been following a car that was hit head on. Everyone in the collision was dead. There were multiple fatalities, including a boy and his father. She was the only one present at the scene, the only witness, and this is why she was arriving late.

Can you imagine? I can hardly think about this to tell you. How does one comfort a person, a stranger in such a moment? I was shaken, and did my best. I listened, and I listened, and I listened. Oh, the horror of it. I can feel it as I write this. Against my own happy arrival there could be no darker contrast. This woman was not a writer, not part of the Women Writers' Retreat, and I spoke to her only once after that evening, but I can tell you it was a sober start to the weekend for both of us.

*****

Sunday evening, July 24th , was a boisterous time in the Boathouse. The Women Writers' Retreat was officially underway, and the Faculty were revealing the time and content of their classes. Participants got to choose two classes: one from 9-10:30 AM and the other from 11-12:30 PM daily.

I was horrified when I learned Jil Hanifan's poetry class conflicted with Carmine Coco-DeYoung's Writing for Children and Young Adults. I'd waited all year to be back with Jil, but I'd also been trying to teach myself to write prose for children, and hoped to study with Carmine. I had the notion that if I could learn to write engaging prose for children, I'd be able to write good prose for anyone. I wanted to write both prose and poetry.

Carmine's class was restricted in size, and she only took students who had some experience writing for children. I wasn't certain she'd receive me as a student. When it came time to sign up for classes, I put my name on both Jil's and Carmine's class lists.

The next morning, I spoke with Carmine in the dining hall. I told her about my winter young adult reading, and showed her a short story I'd written. It was an account of a ten-year-old Catholic girl who begins saying the rosary daily because she wants to ask God to let her see through Jesus's eyes for a moment so she can understand why he didn't hate the people who crucified him. Carmine said she'd be happy to have me in her class, and that's how I ended up missing Jil's poetry class in 2016.

*****

I hardly get any sleep at PLC, and that first Monday morning I was up before dawn, standing alone in front of Marian lodge alongside a large tree stump which had been the perch of a plastic owl in 2015. I'd taken note of the plastic owl because he seemed so incongruous with the wildness of the place, and I'd written about him in my journal.

...the plastic owl keeps his watch, stands at attention upon his tree stump perch below the weathered flagpole; plastic eyes don't blink, nor plastic wings rise for flight; sedentary fellow, faithful sentry, keeps at bay all mice, not men; could not fool a fool; no feathers here, no head that swivels; a ghost of what he might have been, had he not been formed of extruded plastic.

The Plastic Owl Atop His Perch in 2015

"Faithful Sentry, Defends Against All Mice, Not Men"

(Photograph Courtesy of Diane Kavanaugh-Black)

On this 2016, crack of dawn morning, the first day of classes, I was looking out over the lake thick with a rising mist, and thousands of circles of broken water where fish were feeding. I was missing the plastic owl, and thinking of all the precious women writers sleeping around me, considering the truth of life: *nothing lasts forever.*

I used the plastic owl's vacant stump to support my notebook, and began writing this poem.

carp-e-diem

i stand by the stump,
once the plastic owl's perch,
alone in this morning.

well, not exactly alone.

there is a busy ant ascending
my left ankle, and a chorus of birds
sounding off wildly around me.

you are not far away either,
sleeping the best sleep of this night
in your small cabins.

are you dreaming?

can you see the mist on the lake?
and all the circles of broken water
spilling outward from small centers?

it is the time of fishing.

let us go together, you and i.
take our boats out on this water.
cast our lines into this deep.

feel the tug, the pull,
the thrashing weight.
measure our hunger against its own.

can you taste it?
life's fierce will
upon your string?

and when we wake,
shall we release it? watch it
glide back into freedom?

there is nothing to lose now.
nothing to fear. nothing
to do — but feed the fish.

*****

At 6:45 AM I found myself stumbling around in the dark of the dining hall, searching for the light switch. It wasn't in an obvious place. Mission accomplished, I headed for the coffee pots. The directions for making coffee were on the wall above and to the right of the two brewers. Soon enough I had my favorite Hookjaw Charters coffee mug full of the best coffee in the world. It's the water – – not the brand — that makes PLC coffee so special. The water, right out of the tap, anywhere at the camp, is ice cold, clean, pure and delicious. I make it a point to drink gallons of it every day.

Around 7 AM Sr. Monica Murphy, showered and dressed in multicolored, well-worn hospital scrubs arrived to begin her work day.

And now I digress a bit. From day one, of my first experience at Pyramid Life Center I understood it was no ordinary place, and it didn't take me long to recognize what made it so special was Sr. Monica Murphy. She was *the juice, the life, the source of everything that happened at the camp.* She *was* the camp!

I learned that Sr. Monica and two priests, thirty some years ago, had convinced the Diocese of Albany, when they wanted to sell this property, to let them try to make the camp pay for itself by running summer programs like the Women Writers' Retreat. During the winters, Sr. Monica was a guidance counsellor at Catholic Central High School in Troy, New York. Summers she brought select kids, mostly boys, to work at the camp.

I'd paid attention to *'the boys'* last summer going about their chores, and they always seemed at ease and content whatever odd job they were doing: delivering toilet paper to Cabin 4, building something with the visiting carpenter, washing dishes, sweeping out cabins, or driving campers here and there in the golf cart. I'd see them take midday swims, and heard tell of evening runs to Schroon Lake for ice cream.

From my vantage point, the camp seemed to operate with a comfortable ease. I decided these young teenagers, city kids mostly, were living an invaluable lesson about life and work and human happiness under Sr. Monica's tutelage. I wanted to understand more about their relationship with Sr. Monica, and more about Sr. Monica herself.

So that morning, with my Hookjaw Charters coffee mug in hand, I paid close attention to the dining hall routine.

These are my observations as I recorded them in my journal.

Sr. Monica arrives 7 AM. She is in the kitchen. Neil arrives. There is no greeting between them. Sr. Monica simply says "The first thing we need to do…". Luke arrives around 7:05AM. Soon there are four boys and Sarah with Sr. Monica in the kitchen, all moving gracefully, quietly at their tasks. Quiet speech, easy movement, buff young men, gentle as lambs, altogether they are like a seasoned orchestra tuning up. Sr. Monica corrects someone. There is quiet laughter. The dining hall fills with smells and signs of breakfast. There is no extraneous noise. There is a mood of ease and purpose, and I suppose confidence of knowledge, the way one pulls on an old sweater. Something is accomplished with precision, and without conscious effort. Movements familiar, like slipping a foot into an old slipper.

After breakfast, I asked Sr. Monica if I could help wash the lunch dishes that afternoon. I explained I was writing about '*the boys,*' and wanted to have the *kitchen experience.* This was mostly true, I was writing about '*the boys,*' but what I really wanted to understand was their relationship with Sr. Monica.

*****

It felt strange to step into the kitchen. I've always felt it to be Sr. Monica's domain, and a kind off-limits inner sanctum to campers like me. It's easy to see into the kitchen from the main dining hall area, but to enter it felt as if I were visiting a sacred shrine on a mountain in Tibet.

As luck and fate would have it, Luke Geddies was *the* boy in charge of clean up that afternoon. I already knew Luke well from trips around camp last year in the golf cart. When I explained I was here to learn to wash dishes, I'm pretty certain he thought I was nuts, but he was game, and set me to scrubbing.

While we were both working away, and I was getting the hang of loading the dishwasher, Luke and I began to chat. I was excited, and wanted to share with him the incredible experience I'd had that morning writing in Carmine's class.

This is what I told Luke: "Carmine passed around a manila envelope with folded slips of paper, and we each selected one. On it was the name and age of a young person. My slip read, *Anthony, age 13*. Carmine explained that this was *our character* for the week, and asked us to write down everything we already knew about him/her."

I felt like a deer in the headlights, didn't know what I was doing, and wondered if I was in over my head. The women around me immediately set to writing, and I was stunned, wondering how I could possibly do this. How could I know such a thing? But when I began to write I could see him —*this boy named Anthony* — and I knew all about him."

I read Luke what I had written.

Anthony's spending a summer on a ranch with a school chum, named Sam McElroy. His father's been killed in Iraq. He and his widowed mother are living in the suburbs of Las Vegas. Sam's father, Mr. McElroy has invited Anthony to spend time at the ranch while his mother travels east to visit family, and have surgery for her breast cancer which Anthony does not know about.

When I finished my story, I asked Luke —"*Do you wanna try this*!?" and promised, "*You'll be amazed*!"

I wrote down the name of an 18-year-old girl, and handed it to Luke. The next day, he was all about it. He'd had the same miraculous experience I had. Not only could he imagine this character, he already knew all about her; where she lived, what she was doing, and could converse with her at will.

Luke Geddies, Marian Lodge

2016

*****

As I sit here in 2022 writing this memoir, I have twelve chapters of a Young Adult novel tucked away in my filing cabinet. It is the story of *Anthony,* but a funny thing happened. When I got serious about writing his story, I couldn't put a word on paper, so I stopped to have an imaginary conversation with him.

"Anthony, don't you want me to write your story?"

His response: *"My name is Anthony John DeMarco, but nobody in Montana calls anybody Anthony or Tony*, they *call me Jake, for John"*

I heard *Jake* clearly, made him 12 years old, moved him, his mother, Sam, Mr. McElroy and the ranch to Montana, and his story flowed out of my pen onto the page.

Here's a synopsis of Chapter 8 of Jake's Story:

It's June, and 12-year-old Jake and his best friend Sam McElroy are summer hired hands on Sam's father's cattle ranch — the Circle M. Jake and Sam met last fall in the 6th grade at Tipton Academy, and Jake has spent almost every Saturday since at Sam's ranch. Jake wants to be the best horseman on the planet, and Mr. McElroy, with patient instruction, and kind attention has gotten Jake off to a very good start. As Chapter 8 ends, the boys are with a ranch hand named Tomas. It is the end of their second day working on the range as *bona fide* hired hands. A storm has come up, and Tomas, Sam, and Jake are taking cover in a small shed at the base of the windmill/water pump at a place called Big Well.

*****

When I returned home to New Jersey, I shared my story of discovering *Jake* with my neighbor Arlene Marcoe *(aka artistarlene)*. In response, she gifted me this Oil Portrait of a boy she had painted *"years ago"*. It *was* Jake!! Pyramid Magic had followed me home

Here's Jake!! *aka* Anthony Age 13

Carmine Coco-DeYoung, sword in hand, with her 2016 *Writing for Children and Young Adults* class where I met *Anthony, age 13*. On the left, in the red tee shirt is **Kim Trotto**. **Maddy Spadola** is in the peach colored tee shirt next to Carmine, and I'm standing on the far right. The tree stump in the center of the photograph is the former perch of the *Plastic Owl,* where I wrote the poem *carp-e-diem*.

CHAPTER 3

DANCING WITH AUDRE LORDE

JULY 14TH- JULY 21ST
2017

"The fool knows that the only true madness is to regard the world as rational."

William Shakespeare, *King Lear*

In 2017, I talked my writer friend Mary Bilderback into coming to camp with me. I was excited to share Pyramid Life Center and the Women Writers' Retreat with her. I hoped she'd find the same value in it as I had, but I know Mary well, and was ready for her to receive the experience in her own way. What I was certain of, is that she would love the camp, and Pyramid Lake.

Mary is partly the reason I am a writer. She introduced me to the poetry of Mary Oliver in the late 80's, and to the teachings of Pema Chodron soon thereafter. Our adult lives came alongside one another when the two of us found ourselves working in the Biology Department of Georgian Court, a small Catholic women's college, in Lakewood, New Jersey.

I'd say a kind of harmonic set up between us. As fellow biologists, poets, and *humans-only-being* in an incomprehensible universe, we quickly discovered a lot of common ground, including a frequently obverse sense of humor.

Without knowing it, we had shared similar extraordinary childhoods summering on the same barrier island, six miles off the coast of New Jersey, a place called '*LBI*' (Long Beach Island). We didn't know one another then. Mary's family had a cottage on sixth street in Barnegat Light at the north end of the island near the inlet, and my family, my large extended Irish family, favored the south end of the island, around Beach Haven Terrace.

When we arrived at PLC on Friday July 14th, I was so excited to show Mary the camp, I forgot to arrive myself. After we exited the small meditation cabin on the hill overlooking the lake (*I was leaving nothing out*), I chanced to look down on the floating dock where three small sailboats were stabled. My favorite green and white Sunfish caught my eye, and suddenly, without warning, I was seized, convulsed by emotion, and dropped to my knees sobbing. Mary stood by while I cried unashamedly. When I stopped crying I explained, " I just heard the silence." I had arrived.

*****

On the ride north, Mary and I read and considered some of C.D. Wright's poetry. I had thought C.D. Wright was going to be the featured poet in Jil Hanifan's poetry class. It turned out I was wrong, the featured poet was Audre Lorde. Wright had been the featured poet in 2016, the year I missed Jil's class to study with Carmine.

Audre Lorde's poetry took me by storm, and I began to channel her energy. I had the most incredible experience writing a poem entitled *Litany for Wetlands,* after Lorde's *Litany for Survival.* Jil asked us to write a litany using Lorde's line, *"you were never meant to survive."*

On Wednesday morning my *Litany for Wetlands* poem began to arrive with such an intensity I had to actually move to write it. I went down to the basketball court below the dining hall and began shooting baskets. With every new line I wrote, I threw the ball harder and harder, and the poem kept arriving. I couldn't believe what I wrote, or how the poem made me feel. I liked it.

That afternoon, Miriam Russell was holding Open Mic practice sessions in the Boathouse, and I decided I'd try out my new poem with her. Before I tell you more about that, I want you to know Miriam Russell, and our history together.

Miriam Russell was a Miss America Contestant representing New York State in 1958, when I was thirteen years old. In my PLC eyes she was a seasoned veteran of the Women Writers' Retreat, and had a boatload of *bona fides* at the University Level teaching English, Writing, and Public Speaking. What I need you to know is that she was a power-house.

I learned to trust Miriam's Open Mic coaching back in 2015, the year she taught me to pronounce the word *'poem.'* My memory can still hear the two of us in a kind of *Laurel and Hardy* dialogue: Miriam trying to explain to me how to correctly pronounce the word.

" *Poe—em*" she said, "NOT *pome!!* "

That summer afternoon I did my best to hear the difference between the word *'poe-em'* and the word *'pome',* but my brain remained doggedly unconvinced there was a difference, and every time I spoke to say the word *'poe-em'* it came out of my mouth as *'pome'*.

It took me a year to train my brain to move my lips and tongue to utter the sound 'poe-em' correctly. These days I can do it without thinking, but back then, on that Wednesday afternoon in July, all I could think to do was circumvent the matter. I changed my opening words to *"Three short pieces,"* and slipped under Miriam's radar to read my *'pomes'*.

So back to *Litany for Wetlands,* and my 2017 Open Mic practice session with Miriam. I was still channeling Audre Lorde when I entered the Boathouse at 1 PM, and found it full of women working quietly on their journals for Sr. Fran Dempsey's class. Their work involved, not just writing, but painting and collage, and they were into it.

I found Miriam seated across from the podium working quietly with another writer. When it came my turn, I took my place at the podium and began to read my '*poe-em*'. One of the things Miriam had taught me about reading aloud was to underline words or phrases to be given emphasis, and create a script for reading that created a varied pace and tone. I began reading Litany for Wetlands not paying much attention to anything else happening in the room.

I directed my words to Miriam. She didn't interrupt me once, not anywhere along the way, and by the end of my reading, when I spoke the words of my last line "*you were never meant to survive*" I realized everyone in the room had stopped what they were doing, and were listening to me. Miriam asked me to read the poem again, and I did.

By then, I understood the poem was powerful, and was affecting everyone. After the second reading, I got a spontaneous ovation, and lots of well-wishes for my performance that evening. Even Miriam was encouraging me, telling me not to hold back.

You know, I loved the energy of that poem, my heart was in it, resonating with the heart of Audre Lorde.

When I read it that evening in front of almost eighty serious women writers, I nailed it, and they told me so with their enthusiastic applause. I looked out at Miriam and she was smiling broadly, swollen with pride, the kind I imagine an Olympic coach feels after their protégé wins the gold.

I still remember how good it felt to stand there and receive that affirmation. It marked an important milestone in my evolution as a writer. I understood for the first time that words I put on paper actually *have power*. It was like discovering fire. I tell you I haven't been the same since. Learning to control fire. Now that's a life-time's work!

*****

When I returned to New Jersey, I did not share *Litany for Wetlands* with my local poetry writing group, even though I loved it. I understood it was an angry poem, substantially different from the writing I had been doing, or anything anyone else was doing. In 2020, because of the pandemic, the Dodge Poetry Festival was a Virtual Event. I attended, and during the course of the week participated in an Open Mic session. I pulled out *Litany for Wetlands,* made some minor changes, and read it. My Zoom Chat lit up with praise. I'd been heard.

Litany for Wetlands

After Audre Lorde's *"Litany for Survival"*

for all those who live below sea level

twice a day submerged in tide,

wetlands dwellers, with gills and lungs,

amphibians of the sea

for all those who live above and below the surface

guardians of the womb, who understand

like mothers, tides of wet and dry,

fluids amniotic

for all those who would keep the nursery open

for spiders spinning webs, diamond

backs, and blue clawed crabs, grasses

weeping salt

for all those who would come to spawn,

or be spawned in this place —

when they come — to say you're useless

when they come — to say you're no good

when they come — to say you're worthless

when they come — to say you've got to go

when they come — to drain your waters

rip you open, bury you in dry

well… I say…

I say…I say… remember

i say *remember*

i say *remember! remember! remember! remember!*

"you──── were──── never──── meant──── to──── survive"

Edwin B. Forsythe Wildlife Refuge

My Wetlands Home

Miriam Russell, Front Porch of Marian Lodge

2016

Mary did most of her writing on the small dock below Cabins 4 and 5, though she did drop in now and then to Jil Hanifan's class. What she thought about, and wrote on the dock that summer was transmuted into an essay she published in the *Global Sisters Report.* Mary is a RSM, a *Religious Sister of Mercy.* The piece is entitled *I Would Never Help a Worm Cross the Road.*

Here's a taste — with Mary's permission:

"We understand why worms surface in the rain ... they want out of soggy soil. They breathe through their skins and need to be moist, but in too much water they suffocate. On the road it's no picnic either. Desiccation or worse.

But I would never help a worm across the road. Not that I haven't tried. Compassionate techniques include: the stick method, where I sought the perfect stick — not too long and not too prickly — strong enough to carry the weight of a worm.

Once I peeled an oak twig and stuck it strategically under the limp and legless creature before me — on whose behalf I was giving up a sizable chunk of my morning. I lifted and aimed the direction of my rescue at the grass on the south side of the road ... but to which side had the worm been headed in the first place?

And which of its nearly identical ends was the business end in charge of the trip?

Thus, I worried as it dangled from its wooden lifeline until it fell, or jumped, and landed right back where it had been — before help came. It hit the ground in a sort of quizzical shape as if it had positioned itself at the end of the sentence, properly punctuating my philosophical dilemma.

I've also tried the leaf method — snow plow action, approaching client lengthwise. But the worm merely rolled and resisted as if the leaf were why it had left the territory it was fleeing in the first place.

And then there was the combo leaf and stick method — thoughtfully improving the inadequacies of the former protocols — stick for lift, leaf as safety net — as you may have imagined. Results? No additional data. Leaving me with several open-ended questions:

Was this worm meant to cross the road? Was I meant to figure into its survival? Or was this simply a case of serendipity hijacked by misdirected fellow feeling, loaded with urgency by my forethought of tragedy? (Squish …oops.) Or just plain hubris on my part? Who, by the way, had invited me to care? Clearly I did. I do."

The whole of Mary's essay can be found by *googling* the Global Sisters Report. You'll find all Mary's essays there, including this one published August 6th, 2019. They're all delicious, and also nutritious, in that special way we all need to be fed.

Dock Below Cabins 4 and 5

Driving down the long, winding, narrow road, away from the camp with Mary that summer, I was a happy woman in my writer's skin, eager for another year of my writer's life. It had been, as it had always been, a joy to be with these *writerly* women, and I'll tell you a secret – – in my silly mind, PLC remains as ever, a fairy tale place that disappears when I turn left onto the black tar pavement of Route 74, and pops-up again whenever I return to Paradox.

View of the Swimming Area and Boathouse

CHAPTER 4

REST

JULY 13ᵀᴴ – JULY 20ᵀᴴ
2018

Nor would I be a Poet—

It's finer own the ear

Enamored-impotent-content

The license to revere

A privilege so awful

What would the Dower be,

Had I the Art to stun myself

With bolts of melody

Emily Dickinson, #505

My neighbor, Arlene Marcoe (*aka artistarlen*e), came to PLC with me in July, 2018. She hadn't opportunity to go to a summer camp as a child, and when I went on-and-on telling stories, showing pictures of Pyramid Life

Center, and doing my best to relate the happenings of three magical summers, it came naturally to me to ask her if she wanted to go.

She packed her oil paints and easel, a clean notebook, her sleeping bag, clothes, and bathing suit and off we went. Neil assigned us the upstairs room in Cabin 4 with two beds. The room I'd shared with Maddy in 2015.

As we drove north, I had the conversation I've had with all my guests. I told Arlene I needed her to understand how precious my week at the writer's retreat was to me, and while I was honestly happy she was with me, I needed her to know, except for meal times, I was here to write, and needed to be left alone to do whatever my muse was calling me to do. In a nutshell, I was telling her *"You're on your own kid!"*

Arlene eased into the life of the camp without skipping a beat. Every time I saw her, she was engaged with someone or something. She enrolled in several courses, including Cynthia Brackett-Vincent's Weekend Poetry Class, being taught that year in a pinch by Ellen Secci. Together we began writing and sharing haiku, as well as thoughts about what we were both experiencing. In the evenings we spent happy hours lying on our cots reading poetry to one another, laughing, chatting, reviewing the day. We fell into an easy pattern, similar to that of college roommates. Confidences were shared. Her company was delightful.

Indeed, Arlene gave me all the space I needed, and better still, her company fell well within the limits of the plan my muse had for me. In retrospect, I see, she must have been part of the plan, because when my faith in myself as a writer ebbed as on a neap tide, it was Arlene who helped me begin to sort myself out.

Arlene Marcoe, *'aka artistarlene'*

2018

Right from the beginning I was off-balance. There were changes in 2018 I was unprepared to absorb. First of all, poet Jil Hanifan would not be attending. Word was she was taking a break, and would return in 2019. I accepted the report, but had my doubts about Jil's return. There'd been a disagreement at the end of the 2017 retreat involving Jil and a few other women. I wasn't privy to the whole of it, but I knew it had upset Jil. When she didn't arrive I wasn't surprised. I decided she'd made up her mind about something, and I accepted the truth of the possibility she might never be back. I was devastated.

It didn't help matters either that Cynthia Brackett-Vincent was also not attending. I'd come to depend on Cynthia and her Weekend Poets of Pyramid class to get my muse and I sorted out for the week ahead. I've always loved the poets and poetry Cynthia chose to instruct us. I remember in particular my experience of her reading a Jane Kenyon poem, *What Came to Me*. I don't think I'd ever been so moved by a poem. Cynthia's voice and encouraging instruction was another loss I'd have to absorb.

On Friday evening, I hadn't realized Cynthia's poetry class had been moved to the main room of the lodge, and entered the Fireplace Room like a robot. I walked straight into the middle of an *AL-Anon* session in full swing, and was well into the room when I understood the situation. I was embarrassed and apologized profusely. My predicament was met with sympathy, and I was redirected to the main room in the lodge. I entered that room off-balance and, indeed, later in the weekend I'd wished I stayed in the *AL-Anon* group.

You see — in 2018— I arrived with things weighing on me. My older sister Barbara had died in Pittsburgh, Pennsylvania on Holy Saturday, March, 31st. She was 75 years old, and her death was unexpected. Her death certificate stated the cause of death as cardiac arrest and starvation. Yes — in the *'Year of our Lord 2018,'* in the United States of America, *my sister — died of starvation.*

I won't go into the details of her dying, but suffice it to say, through the 20:20 lens of hindsight, I was waking up to the fact that my sister may have been, in fact had likely been, anorexic nearly her entire adult life. There were other complications around her death, but I couldn't shake the stark truth that no one, myself included, ever managed to see what may have been happening to her for years.

Among the women writers, I knew I had friends who could enlighten me about anorexia, and I was eager to speak with them. I spent hours with therapist and songwriter Debra Burger one evening, chatting well into the post-midnight hours trying to wrap my head around the idea.

I could recall a summer day when my sister and I were in our forties or early fifties, she'd told me proudly she could wear a size 4. I couldn't stop asking myself, why,

why, why hadn't I thought this strange? A size 14, a 12, a 10, or even an 8 would have been more reasonable for her height. She was tall.

My sister and I loved each other, of that I have no doubt, but in the end, I had to admit we were strangers. It seemed all my losses were converging in the 2018 Women Writers' Retreat, and oh, what a time it was.

*****

In the Boathouse Sunday evening, I signed up for Sandi Dollinger's playwrighting class, and indeed, it turned out to be the perfect antidote to my uneven, dreary mood.

Before I tell you my experience in Sandi's class, I want you to know I'd taken note of Sandi in 2015, because I thought she was Mary Oliver — *the poet*. I know that sounds ridiculous, but the first time I saw Sandi I was sitting behind her at an Open Mic, and she was wearing a broad brimmed khaki hat similar to one's I'd seen Mary Oliver wear in photographs. In my breathless wonder, and naiveté as a newbie, I believed Sandi *was* Mary Oliver.

Sandi Dollinger, Playwright *Extraordinaire*

I mention this case of mistaken identity because again it demonstrates the esteem in which I held the *writerly* women I saw around me in 2015. Now that I know Sandi, I realize she's every bit the genius writer Mary Oliver was, only she writes plays. I count it a privilege to be in Sandi's classes, and make it a point to sign up for every session she teaches.

Sandi's 2018 playwriting class was held in the Chapel, and it opened with Sandi speaking about *longing.* Sandi told us, *"to write plays we would have to understand the deepest longings of our characters."* She defined the word longing, and then asked us to write down a longing of our own.

I wrote a short sketch about my experience of this class, for the 2018 Women Writers' Retreat Anthology.

A Summer Sketch

"...to rest is to give up on the already exhausted will as the prime motivator of endeavor, with its endless outward need to reward itself through established goals" David Whyte, Consolations

What slithers onto the shore of my summer memory is a writing prompt: one offered at the beginning of my mid-July Adirondack Women Writers' Retreat.

"To write a play you must understand longing," the playwright, who reminds me always of Mary Oliver, begins. *"Great plays are built on the longings of their characters."*

My mind snaps to attention.

"A longing is not a want, or a wish. Not even a desire. It's something more remote. A soul's deep yearning — perhaps for something unattainable."

I understand exactly what is being spoken of.

"Write down a longing you have."

In this sacred place, among these women, I trust myself. Still, I am afraid. Uncertain I want to know what I long for. Uncertain what I might need do if I had such knowledge.

Alone inside myself, I pause. Breathe in the rare, delicious mountain air. Allow myself to come into my body. To feel the concentration, the effort being made by the women around me. I take up my pencil, commit to the task, and bend myself toward it.

Fearless in my writer's skin, I open to hear a word forming, rising within me.

At first, it is a sound so faint, so far away I can barely hear it. And then like a gentle rolling wave it washes up at my feet: *whole, complete and perfect.*

The word is *Rest.* I long for — *Rest.*

The fact catches me by surprise. I am at once relieved and amazed with the truth of my discovery. I smile in the mirror of my mind, and feel peals of laughter erupt in my soul. I am a coyote baying at the moon.

I write: *I long for rest — a soul deep rest. The kind I feel after laughing so hard I cry, or crying so hard, I arrive weightless, at the end of tears, on the arid flatland of a bottomless sorrow.*

I'm delighted, and make an executive decision. This year, I will use my precious time at writer's camp, among these women, *to rest!*

*****

Rest is what I did at the 2018 Women Writers' Retreat. By that I mean I made no effort to *accomplish* anything. I attended Sandi's class, and after that it was all improvisation. Here is an unedited journal entry from July 2018.

In the dining hall at PLC fifteen minutes before breakfast. There are eleven writers in silence, working as they say in the biz. I've repaired the nosepiece on my glasses, and feel quite accomplished. I'm trying to convince myself it's ok to be me— the way I can be when I'm at rest, I mean "let myself go," not drift exactly, certainly NOT that— but be free to let the past be past and the future be who knows what? It's a spiritual journey this trip. I woke up this morning thinking "half myself is underdeveloped." I have a strong front and no glutes; my posterior body, the whole half of me is undeveloped. It needs my intention and attention.

This brief scribble was prescient because 2018 morphed into what can only be called a spiritual journey. On Tuesday morning I descended the staircase in Cabin 4, swung open the closed door at the bottom, and stepped into the living room space with my head up and eyes looking straight ahead.

What I saw was something that looked like a large insect, perhaps a praying mantis on the screen of the window that opens onto the porch. Naturally I was curious and stepped toward it. Slowly it came to me it wasn't a praying mantis, but rather a bronze metal, slender, crucified *Jesus* without a cross: *a 'stick Jesus.'* I took it into my hand. It lay there gently in my palm, a perfect weight, and without too much thought, I decided to take it with me. I put it in my pocket and carried it with me the entire week.

At the end of the week, as I was returning to Cabin 4 to

meet Arlene and load the car, I was walking alone along the wide trail that runs beside the lake. It was a bright sunny day and the wind was blowing strong. The shadows of the leaves above the trail were dark and dancing, dappling the ground in front of me. I took out my new *iPhone,* and began to make a video of my walk, stopping now and then to look out onto the lake. At one point I took the '*stick Jesus'* out of my pocket, and held it in the palm of my hand, allowing the sunlight to fall directly on it. I was making up my mind whether or not I would keep it.

Now this question was no small one for me. I have created in my own mind and in my own way a particular relationship with PLC which involves a strict kind of integrity, which would be offended by walking off with anything. I could, of course, have asked Sr. Monica if I could keep it, and I believe she would have likely said yes, but in the end I decided to put the '*stick Jesus'* back where I found it, leave it for someone else to find. Whatever '*stick Jesus's'* fate, it's not for me to know. What I can say is this — I'll never forget the way *he* rested in my hand that week, and glowed like heaven itself in the dappled summer light.

*****

It was at the farewell campfire on Thursday evening when I missed Jil Hanifan the most. In my heady first three PLC Women Writers' Retreats, Jil had been a huge presence, a stoker of all sorts of fires in me, and in the finales of each of these weeks she had stepped into the circle at the closing campfire to become the orchestrator, and leader of our sad and sacred farewells.

She would end our closing ceremony by calling us to dance the *Hokey Pokey* together, a song which to my open ear and soul, sounded like a writer's solemn prayer.

Put your whole self in —

take your whole self out

Put your whole self in —

n' shake it all about

Do the Hokey Pokey

n' turn yourself around

That's What It's All About!

For me, camp week seems to pass like a single breath. In the rhythms and movements of our dancing to this silly rhyme I hear Jil's finest lesson to me, a coded message on how to live my life as a poet/writer: *"put your whole self in — take your whole self out — put your whole self in — that's what it's all about!!"* No one can lead the *Hokey-Pokey* like Jil, but at every last campfire — I step up and send my own version of that silly prayer to heaven! *"Hokey Pokey!!"*

Carol Whitlow, Creating the Fabulous Pyramid Boutique

CHAPTER 5

THE END OF THE BEGINNING

JULY 12TH – JULY 19TH
2019

"There is no measuring time, a year doesn't matter, and ten years are nothing. Being an artist means, not reckoning and counting, but ripening like the tree which does not force its sap and stands confidently in the storms of spring, not afraid that afterward summer may not come. It does come. But it comes only to those who are patient, who are there as if eternity lay before them, so unconcernedly silent and vast."

Rainer Maria Rilke, *Letters to a Young Poet*

Many women at the PLC Women Writers' Retreat will tell you they wait all year to return for another week of writing in July. I am one of them. And so you can imagine my frustration in 2019 when I couldn't seem to get on the road to head north. I was ready enough to leave the morning of Friday, July 12th. Dominic, my Border Collie mutt was taken care of, and the car was packed – – *loaded* I'd say. I had Arlene's husband, my neighbor Woods Davis, tie an almost brand-new paddle board on the roof rack the night before.

The board was a gift from my brother Mike and his wife Susie in 2015, the summer following my mastectomy. They figured it would help my recovery, and it would have, had I liked paddle boarding. I live on a tidal creek, and it could have been just the ticket, but I didn't take to it, not at all. I like to row, and sail, and swim, but paddle boarding, not so much! Anyway, I decided to take the paddle board to camp with me. I figured someone would want it, or I could give it to the camp.

I drove out my driveway around 7:30 AM figuring on an arrival in Paradox around 3 or 3:30 PM, but hadn't gone two miles before I had a problem with my car, a 2012 Hyundai Touring. It was a stuck rear brake caliper, and I was told the part would have to come from a Hyundai dealer. "*It could take all day*", the mechanic said, "*or even two.*"

I was so bummed. I had waited all year to go to PLC, this just couldn't be happening! I'd had my car serviced in June, made all the preventive repairs, even new spark plugs. I was a whiny, miserable specimen sitting in the waiting room of my mechanic that morning.

Sometime around 10:30 AM the mechanic stood in front of me and said "*it's done.*"

Whoa, done!? I could hardly believe the man. All this time I'd thought we were waiting for a part! Done, sounded to my ears like my mechanic had walked on water.

Wow, I was going to get to camp! Late, but I'd get there!

I was anxious when I finally got on the Garden State Parkway, picked up speed, testing the car with the paddle board on the roof. I had visions of the paddle board flying off and killing someone behind me. A few miles at 60 mph, slower than cruising speed in New Jersey, I started to relax, everything seemed fine. I was blessing Woods in my mind, and revising my ETA: with one gas stop, I'd be in Paradox in time for dinner. That, as it turned out, was overly optimistic.

Did I mention it was a *freakin'* hot day. The temperature in NJ was circling 100 degrees, at least that's what my car's outdoor temperature gauge was reading. It was the kind of day when asphalt softens. It was cool enough inside my car, and I was feeling lucky my air conditioning was in good order, when I noticed a light I'd never seen before lit up on my dashboard.

TPMS, uhm, what's that? I wondered. *Well, the car's running, it's NOT the engine! What is it!?*

I was using the Express Lanes of the Garden State Parkway, going what felt like a million miles an hour, with no place to pull over. Traffic was heavy and fast, and no nearby rest stops. My mind was spinning around the letters TPMS — '*T— P — M — S,*' and then it occurred to me, TP was tire pressure.

Yikes, the heat of the road, the paddle board on the roof: *Are my tires going flat? Or are they over-inflating?* Hot air expands, and I had visions of my tires exploding. I decided to tough it out till the next service area south of the Perth Amboy Bridge, but as I approached the bridge, I said *"hell no, too hot to stop,"* and made up my mind to go for it.

The light on the dashboard went off somewhere over the NJ-NY border, but came back on again on the Northway a few miles north of Glens Falls. When I exited at Severance, it was 5PM. I headed for the nearest gas station, turned a couple of dollar bills into quarters, added air to all four tires, and read the gauge. 32 *psi all around*! *Good to go!*

I was at the camp by 5:30 PM hugging poet/writer, PLC good buddy, Diane Kavanaugh-Black in the parking lot. Diane got a look at the paddle board, and *voila* it had found its new home. Exhausted, relieved, and happy, I began the 2019 Women Writers' Retreat.

*****

In the days leading up to the retreat I'd been busy putting the finishing touches on a book I authored, and was about to publish using Amazon's Kindle Direct Publishing platform. I'd put the book together in the previous three weeks, and on July 11th, the day before I got into the car to drive north to Paradox, I received a proof copy.

It was my first book, and it didn't have much text, so the word *authored* hardly seems accurate. You see, it was an assemblage of original art and poetry from a very cool Annual Art and Poetry Exhibit at the New Jersey, Ocean County, Long Beach Island Public Library, called *Painted Poetry*.

Work for this *Exhibit* begins in mid-March when local poets and artists submit original works, and sixteen poets and artists are selected by jury to participate in the August-September event. Selected poets and artists are paired at random, and given a month to create a new poem or painting interpreting their partners original work. In mid-August there is a public reception for the artists and poets, in which poets read ekphrastic poems while the paintings are displayed on a large screen.

It's all quite wonderful, and I was the Poetry Coordinator for the Exhibit in 2019, that's how it fell to me to write the book. Well, you can imagine how I felt arriving at the retreat with a proof copy of my first book in hand. As it turns out, there was an impromptu how to publish session during the retreat hosted by Miriam Russell. I was invited, and took my proof copy of *Painted Poetry VI* to the session, where I spread the good news, "*If I can do this anyone can!*"

*****

Later in the week, a little before 9 AM I was racing from the hinterlands of Cabin 5 to Sandi Dollinger's playwriting class in the chapel. It was a perfect cool, blue-skyed morning. When I passed the flower gardens, grass and sand alongside the half-moon bathing beach, I chanced to see Gwen Marable and Jane Eagles sitting by the lake together, engrossed in conversation. I skipped along hardly taking note, until I was nearly to the Boathouse, and then, for some reason stopped dead in my tracks to look back.

What I saw was an iconic scene. Two venerable, older writer women, casually dressed, deep in conversation, notebooks opened, present in the morning, present to each other, with time enough to do the anything or nothing that wants doing on such a splendid day at PLC.

All the hurry inside me fell away and I abandoned any idea of getting to class on time, or getting to class at all. What I wanted was to experience the moment. To see what I saw, and consider the wonder of the miracle we women give ourselves as writers, when we come to this place: *to find the space to hear our own voice, to find a home for our own particular and peculiar selves, and to know and be known in a community of serious women writers.*

I never made it to Sandi's class. I walked back and signaled to Gwen and Jane. Asked if I could take their picture. They agreed, and soon it was the three of us, sitting on the beach that splendid July Adirondack morning. The three of us, talking writing and life.

Gwen Marable and Jane Eagles

July, 2019

*****

When I left Gwen and Jane it was too late to go to class, so I headed for the dining hall and a cup of coffee. I met Sr. Monica at the coffee station along the back wall of the dining hall. She was holding up a grubby looking coffee pot, and immediately began to explain to me that she'd "*ordered glass*," but somehow the four new pots she received "*were plastic*." With that, she opened the door to the broom closet and whipped out a gallon jug of Chlorine bleach. She poured some into one of the pots and began to swirl it. I followed her lead, took another pot, and did the same. There we were, the two of us, swirling plastic coffee pots of bleach at ten in the morning. I never saw anything so effective in cleaning a stained plastic coffee pot in my life, and Sr. Monica was grinning from ear to ear. It was as if we'd pulled off the greatest magic trick of the great Houdini.

It's a rare occasion to have Sr. Monica to yourself for any amount of time, and in the heady moment of our victory over the grunge of the coffee pots, I dared to tell her what I have known from the start, that "*she is Pyramid Life Center*." That her vision, thirty years ago, was the bedrock, the foundation upon which the Women Writers' Retreat was built.

With tears in my eyes, I showed her the proof copy of my *Painted Poetry* book. In my too awkward way, I begged her to have it, as a gift, my small way of thanking her for giving me a place where I could come to know myself as a writer and poet.

This is what I remember inscribing on the cover page.

"It is because of you, and Pyramid Life Center, and the Women Writers' Retreat, that I first dared call myself a writer, and not just that, have come to bravely live my life as a writer and poet."

I also inscribed this haiku.

as through a membrane

i pass into these woods again

my wilderness womb

*****

On Fridays after lunch when it's time to leave PLC, I dilly-dally. Even though I have a long ride home, I don't push myself. I don't rush. I take the time I need to gather the week's lessons inside myself for the winter ahead.

At PLC, I believe in *natural rising, natural living,* and *natural leaving.* After all, PLC is a magical place, and my tardiness exiting has won me several great experiences.

In 2017, Mary Bilderback and I, taking our leave, stopped to fill some jugs with PLC water to take back to New Jersey. When we stepped out of the dining hall there was some commotion. A gigantic, and I mean gigantic snapping turtle was immobile underneath a parked car. Tracy, the resident Life Guard, was attempting to coax it out with a stick so the driver of the car could get underway. Well, Mary and I jumped right into this scene. Somehow the three of us got that monster to crawl out, turn herself, and head at her own very reptilian pace toward the beach. Her terrestrial waddle was really something to see!

Mary eventually named that snapper, *The Paleozoic Immensity,* in an essay entitled L*ogos — Never Uttered the Same Way Twice*, which she published in the *Global Sisters Report* in November, 2019. With Mary's permission, here's a snippet of that fine essay.

"I've never seen a Snark or a Boojum, nor a turtle full-bodied on the banks here, but this summer as I was leaving a camp in upstate New York, a snapping turtle the size of a small goat galumphed across the driveway — between parked, packed cars — toward Pyramid Lake.

Those of us about to get into cars to drive home stood stock still, and watched as she hauled her '*Paleozoic immensity'* back into the murky silence of her liquid lair — ah, those very refreshing waters she had permitted us to swim in — with her. O! With her. And surely others belonging to her underworld tribe — our distant reptilian kin.

It is dark and silent down there (if we dare to look and listen) in the biological underworld from whence we came with mud on our faces and algal hair slung emerald-silken and slimy around our necks, poking our innocent noses up into an air we didn't know we could breathe, into a light that had been waiting for us, starlight beckoning stardust up: "Up, friend, come higher."

That age-old, re-sounding injunction to which we are still responding with varying degrees of intention and grace."

I turned to Tracy, and asked "have we been swimming with this thing all week?"

"Yes," she said " but don't worry, it won't hurt you, unless of course, *you dangle your feet off the float."*

I tucked that piece of information in the back of my brain, and good I did, because in 2019, on the hottest day of the hottest days of July, with humidity enough to turn everything to mush, Diane Kavanaugh-Black and I met the *Paleozoic Immensity* herself, in a close encounter, of a *dangling feet* kind.

We were seated on the edge of the dock below Cabins 4 and 5, not just dangling, but swinging our bare-feet back and forth, cooling ourselves in the splash of the water. It was the heel of my right foot she bumped first, and my ignorant foot said to my brain…

… "it's *just —a loose board.*"

But when Diane and I both nearly simultaneously saw the *snapper* of our worst nightmare, and in panic jumped to our feet, screaming and hugging one another at the center of the dock, I couldn't stop repeating, over and over again —

"Tracy told me! Tracy told me! Don't dangle your feet!"

To our amazement the *Paleozoic Immensity* herself, was unfazed by all this ruckus. Cool as a cucumber she turned to look Diane and me straight in the eye. She stared. We stared. All this staring allowed us to appreciate the true majesty of this living relic, and enough time for Diane to locate her camera, take aim, and capture this photograph.

Her Majesty

The Paleozoic Immensity

2019

Photographer, Poet/Writer, North Woods Naturalist, **Diane Kavanaugh-Black** (foreground) and **Maddy Spadola** enjoying a Sunday afternoon break between the Weekend Poets of Pyramid Class and the beginning of the 2018 Women Writers' Retreat

*****

I was *the last of the last* of the Women Writers to leave PLC in 2019. The camp was empty when I began my walk from the dining hall to cabin 5 to retrieve my packed car. I was surprised when I ran into Nan Payne driving down the hill alongside Marian lodge with her kayak strapped to her roof. She rolled down her window and called out to me.

"I'm glad it's you!" she said.

I looked back at her, and knew exactly what she was saying. It's hard leaving PLC, and she was glad it was me she'd be seeing last. The feeling was mutual.

Somehow, I've come to believe that nothing happens to me at PLC by accident. Everything, good, bad, and indifferent, everyone I meet, everyone I don't meet, all of it feels orchestrated by my muse. And, whatever happens when *I'm leaving*, well, that is *very* special, a kind of *last rite.*

Nan and I are friends, but we don't hang out a lot together at camp. She's a kind of *back woods loner*, and I'm well… I'm a kind of *high plains drifter.* So our meeting seemed especially notable. Nan knows I think for myself and have courage, and I know these same things about her. I think of our friendship as a kind of fine whiskey, a perfect blend of mutual respect and amusement.

Nan is a storyteller, and a storytelling instructor at PLC. She is an iconic, familiar figure at the Thursday night farewell campfires, where she opens closing ceremonies with a story enacted in the shadow and light of a roaring fire.

In 2016, I enrolled in Nan's Storytelling class. It was the year I took Carmine Coco-DeYoung's Writing for Children and Young Adults course. I was eager to learn to tell stories with my prose writing, and thought, *"what better place to hone one's storytelling skills than in a storytelling class."*

As I think back, it was a very brave thing I did to sign up for Nan's class. I knew it then, and I know it now as I write this. Storytelling of the sort Nan is expert, is a kind of high-wire act. It requires one to step out of the crowd, make oneself visible, enter into a contract, a promise with strangers, that says, *" Listen up everybody, I've got something important to tell you, something worth hearing, something worth your precious time and attention."*

It's a big ask, a big promise, and a great responsibility to be a storyteller. It takes trust in one's self and the goodness of others. It's a genuine leap of faith. You see when I say it this way, you understand the boldness and courage it requires, especially as a novice, to do this sort of thing. It takes a lot of practice and experience to be good at it: a lot of *at bats, with the bases loaded*!

This is a photograph of me in 2016, taken immediately after I told my first story in Nan's class. It was the story of the ten-year-old Catholic girl who wanted to ask God for *the favor of seeing with Jesus's eyes*. I can tell you with precision the feelings I was having when this photograph was taken. It was a perfect mix: a fifty-fifty ratio of *pride and relief*.

Nan Payne, Master Storyteller, '*back woods loner*' in the Boathouse

2016

*****

Nan and I didn't know when we said goodbye that Friday afternoon in 2019, that things at PLC would never be the same again. You see, we could not have dreamt it, or even believed what was just over the horizon.

When the news came in August that Sr. Monica Murphy had been killed in a head-on collision on Route 74, it was an impossible thing to grasp: *a world without Sr. Monica in it?— a PLC without Sr. Monica directing it?*

Nor could we have foreseen, or even conceived of a global pandemic: a life-threatening misery which would keep us all from returning to PLC and the Women Writers' Retreat until July, 2022.

As much as I'd like to think we have some control over our fate, we actually don't. I mean we live daily, and have to live daily within the shared illusion there is a *"tomorrow, and tomorrow, and tomorrow."* You know, that *"petty pace"* Will wrote about?

It's the only sane way to ensure the bills are paid on time, and the dog gets fed, but if truth be told, our individual lives have been, and always will be, a rather *contingent affair*.

At 77, I eat this truth with my breakfast every morning, and feel lucky to be around in the evening to digest it. I do my best not to ignore, or predict any of the myriad potential details of my future. Life has taught me that time and trouble arrive on their own schedule.

These days I keep the door to my future wide open. After all, that's how I ran into Maddy and found my way to the PLC Women Writers' Retreat to discover myself a writer. And this memoir you are reading, and I am finishing in *writerly* amazement — well, this I believe, is a kind of punctuation mark, like a period — marking *'the end' of the beginning of my writer's life!*

The End

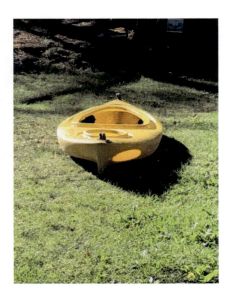

Afterword

I returned to PLC in early **September, 2019** to attend the ***First PLC Writerfest***, a new co-ed writers retreat created by Ellie O'Leary and Nelle Stanton, both long-term veterans of the Women Writers' Retreat. On the final morning of that event, I cried uncontrollably, in great waves, while listening to the hymn *Laudate Omnes Gentes* (Taize) being played in the dining hall in remembrance of Sr. Monica. I was told it was her *favorite hymn.* The English translation is *"Praise God all ye Nations, Praise God!"*

Praise God — Praise God indeed! is what I was thinking*!* Praise God, for Pyramid Life Center, the Women Writers' Retreat, and Sr. Monica Murphy's life!

*****

Because of the Covid Pandemic the **2020 PLC *Women Writers' Retreat* was a Virtual Event,** conducted via Zoom. I participated by hosting a day-long Zoom Meeting in a wild, *hair-brained scheme* to re-create a single day at Pyramid Life Center using gazillions of videos, a lot of audio, and photographs of the Women Writers' Retreat 2015-2019.

Here is the pitch I made to the PLC Women Writers' Retreat Executive Committee to allow me to use Monday, July 20th, from 7 AM- 9 PM to create and host a Virtual Day at PLC

Using Music, Video/Audio/ Slide Presentations, and plenty of Real-Life Shenanigans, Sue Cummings aims to Create a Memorable and Super Virtual Day at PLC. She'll make you feel like your feet are walking the sacred grounds you love. Meet and greet new and old friends. Activities all day long. Drop-In, Drop-out, Drop-in again. Zoom Meeting OPEN at 7AM. Schedule of Activities to Follow — including *Dancing As If No One Is Watching, Singing As If No One Is Listening,* the first ever *Virtual Pyramid Boutique,* a *Susan Glaspell Play* (Trifles), *Interviews with live Poets, Prosers, Storytellers, and a very special Mystery Guest.* **Writing all Day Long — Open Mic 7-9 PM. Breakfast at 8, Lunch at 12:30, and Dinner at 6, don't be late!**

And here are my memories of that day.

It was a hoot-and-a-half! I opened the morning with the Stylistics singing "*You Make Me Feel Brand New*" and **Becky O'Neil** led us in stretches, and we all danced, and laughed, and fell into each-others *virtual arms*.

Lin Murphy sang the PLC Blessing before breakfast. We ate together, did some writing, and shared what we wrote.

At 10*ish* I interviewed **Mary Cuffe-Perez**, author of *Skylar, Nothing by Name*, and my favorite memoir, *Barn Stories*. I'd prepared to speak with Mary by re-reading all her books, and when we got rolling, I felt like I was Terri Gross on NPR Radio. I really enjoyed showcasing Mary's writing, and the two of us had a great conversation.

Carol Whitlow conducted the *first ever* Virtual PLC Boutique. We exchanged stories of things we'd bought and sold at the boutique, and ran around our houses retrieving said items to show one another. It was amazing how we brought alive the wonder, energy and magic of those special shopping days in the dining hall.

Our mystery guest was **Natalie Goldberg,** speaking about *Writing Down the Bones (WDB)*, on a video Prajna Studio's allowed me to share. I'd just completed an on-line writing course with Natalie, and led everyone in a *mini WDB's Writing Practice session, including breakouts for Reading/Listening.*

Bev Skoll was Mrs. Hale, **Arlene Marcoe** was Mrs. Peters, **Mei Stone** was County Attorney Henderson, **Kathy O'Brien** was Sheriff Henry Peters, and **Ellie O'Leary** was farmer Lewis Hale in the great 1916 classic play, *Trifles* **(A Jury of One's Peers)** by Susan Glaspell.

I read the stage directions for the play, and it was going smashingly well, when suddenly I lost my place. Oh, it was a terrible moment for me and everyone listening. I couldn't figure out where we were, and I was scrambling to find my place when I heard **Arlene Marcoe** pick up the narration. In the true spirit of live-theater, the show went on, and all the actors went forward, never skipping a beat.

I was horrified by my misstep, and desperate when I heard my fellow thespians come to my rescue. What comradery it was to do that play together!! To *swim out onto the sea of anything can happen and return safely to shore!*

At 3 PM **Undine Giguere**, writer-storyteller, narrated *The Gruffalo,* a magnificent children's short story about managing troubling fears. She used an animated cartoon version of the story she found on *YouTube* to illustrate the story she was bringing to life with her words. It was wonderful!

We took a well-earned break between 4 and 6 PM, and came back with another great interview. This one with poet **Sara 'with an h' Sullivan**.

After a full-days' pandemic work as an MD, Sarah arrived to read poetry. She read several original poems, and told us about the poets who've most influenced her writing. She shared thoughts on living a poet's life, and hung out with us in the Zoom space answering questions, while we all *inhaled and exhaled poetry*.

At 7 PM everyone was welcomed to the finale, an **OPEN MIC** reminiscent of evenings at the Pyramid Life Center Boathouse. We had a fine time of it, closing the day at almost 9 PM with **Andre Bocelli** singing **Fall on Me** in English and Italian.

It was like being held in the most reassuring, loving embrace of my PLC Sisters, a perfect end to a perfect day! I fell into bed that night exhausted, relieved, and happy. I felt like I'd experienced a real day at PLC in the company of the amazing women who create and recreate the PLC Women Writers' Retreat. Yes, it was virtual, but real enough for me! I had felt the magic, and I prayed others had felt it too!

*****

In **September 2021**, I returned to Pyramid Life Center to attend the ***Second Annual PLC Writerfest***. We were in Covid mode at that retreat, and I remember the dining hall, with a new floor, new round tables, and a refreshment corner with iced lemonade and iced tea. Brian, the new director of PLC, served meals from behind a plastic shield at the end of the dining hall nearest the kitchen. It was, as always, great to be at the camp, but the social distancing and mask requirements were a constant reminder of the real world circling around us.

*****

The **2022 PLC Women Writers' Retreat,** was the *first in-person* retreat since 2019. I had planned to attend, but on July 9th a conversation broke out among participants of my Saturday, Writing Down the Bones (WDB's) Writing Practice Group warning of the highly infectious, vaccine evading *B-variants* of Covid.

Gwen Marable, Diane Kavanaugh-Black, and Undine Giguere, all passionate Women Writers' Retreat veterans, were present to hear this conversation, and when it was over we stayed behind in the Zoom space to discuss what we'd heard.

Gwen and I had plans to travel together to PLC. We were going to drive north from my home in New Jersey on Friday, July 15th so we could attend **Marni Gillard's** ***Weekend Storytelling Workshop***, prior to the Women Writers' Retreat.

I'm a healthy 77, and Gwen is a spry 89, but we both understood the trip was a heavy lift even without the concern of Covid. When the two of us admitted our vaccinations and boosters were not going to protect us, well — we decided our continued good health was a priority, and we ought err on the side of caution. It was an awful decision to make, and left us both feeling disappointed in the extreme.

When I called **Maddy Spadola** to let her know I wouldn't be coming to PLC, she understood, and decided to cancel her own reservation.

Diane was hesitant about the risks of attending, and Undine too. Diane chose to cancel, and Undine, after consultation with her doctors, decided to go for it.

In consequence of our shared disappointment, **Diane Kavanaugh-Black, Gwen Marable, Maddy Spadola, and I** decided to create a *"make-it-up as we go along"* virtual 2022 Women Writers' Retreat.

We met four times via Zoom: Monday, July 18th for breakfast, Wednesday July 20th for lunch around noon, and again in the Evening for an Open Mic with my Barnegat Poets' Society group. On Friday evening, July 22nd, we met for a farewell supper, and virtual campfire.

In the first hours of our disappointment **Gwen** wrote this poem entitled ***Unpacking Pyramid.*** It perfectly sums up our shared feelings about missing the in-person Retreat.

Unpacking Pyramid

Make real lemonade

out of a real, yellow lemon.

Make it slowly.

What's the hurry?

Roll it around, feeling and watching the yellow roundness,

Soft under the skin of the palm of your hand,

Massaging, press it as you roll,

Releasing the cells of what's holding together,

Smell deeply the cup of your hand.

Slice the lemon down the middle slowly,

Inhaling the citrusy clean air surrounding you as you breathe,

Smell your hand, smell your fingers, taste your fingers, they're yours.

Look at the inside of the lemon.

Be Georgia O'Keefe,

Noticing the sweet flower petal of each part,

Each part made up of tiny lemon drops, interior part

Some already bursting with their goodness.

Squeeze half a lemon's goodness

aiming the center of the lemon over the lemon juice squeezer,

no longer regretting the fact that you donated your electric one to unclutter your counter.

You wouldn't trade this silent ritual.

Twisting your wrist,

Feeling the strength of your muscles

strain up to your shoulder.

Relax. What's the hurry?

Pour the juice of each half into the pitcher.

Spoon out the lemon pith left in the rind.

Add it to the juice. Add two glasses of water.

Sweeten to taste with real Domino Sugar, not honey.

Stir and taste.

Place two ice cubes in the glass.

Fill the glass with lemonade.

Now you're ready to unpack your pretty camp sheets

and make your bed here.

Take a sip of lemonade, toasting,

"Here's to some juicy writing!"

*(Printed with permission of the author, Gwen Marable)

*****

On Wednesday afternoon, Maddy put us onto a great writing prompt. She explained she'd been writing memories of her life to leave for her children, grandchildren, and great-grandchildren, and then she added *"no one will likely be interested in what I write, but at least it will be there if they want it."*

I asked Maddy how she might feel if she could hold her mother's memoir in her hands at this very moment?

Well, that question got us *all* to thinking? Asking ourselves *whose memoir we would give anything to read!* We did a quick write, creating a list of people whose memoirs we'd like to *hold in our hands.*

This was followed by a longer write, choosing one person from our list, and imagining what we might discover by reading their memoir. We shared our writing with one another, and were dumbfounded by what we'd written.

I wrote about my maternal Great Great Aunt Mary Elizabeth Barker (1872-1961), who I met in 1950 when I was five years old living in Erie, Pennsylvania.

I remembered she wore rimless glasses, a black dress, black stockings, and her thin wispy white hair was held by bobby-pins in a bun under a thin black hair net. I could recall our being together in my backyard one spring day, while she placed glass jars over young flowers to protect them from a late frost. I had a very specific recollection of her eyes, and the warm feeling and kindness I saw in them. I realized I had loved her.

My sister Barbara, spent more than 12 years before her death, researching, writing, and bringing up-to-date a genealogy and history of our family. After our Zoom session ended, I got my sister's book off the shelf and looked-up my Great Great Aunt Mary.

Her black clothing was explained by the fact that early in her life she'd been a Sister of St. Clare, a contemplative order of the Catholic Church, and later an Episcopalian nun. She'd also been a pediatric dentist. *The first,* or *one of the first* women to graduate with a dental degree from the University of Pennsylvania. She'd spent her life as a missionary in Puerto Rico.

Wow Maddy! What a prompt! Oh, how I'd love to read my Great Great Aunt Mary's Memoir!!! *"Thank you Maddy, Gwen, and Diane, for that great afternoon of writing!"*

*****

Wednesday evening, Diane, Gwen , and I attended my local Barnegat Poets' Society Meeting via Zoom. It was our make-shift version of the Women Writers' Retreat *Open Mic.*

Gwen read her new *Un-Packing Pyramid* poem, I read the section of my PLC Writer's Memoir about my 2015 class with Jil Hanifan, including my poem *The Wrongest Answer*, and Diane read her new poem, entitled *Zinnias*.

Zinnias

Unlock the door

click-thunk.

Enter the heat warily

Sniff the air for dead mice

Listen for wasp intruders

Smell only warm old wood.

Gaze on zinnias

crazy-haired,

crisp curled petals

not lush pink,

not glowing gold

anymore.

Two days before

eight zinnias gleamed green-stalked

wrapped in brown paper

cut ends dripped

on the quick walk back

from the farmers market

(that bustle of unmasked throngs)

While white-snouted I

won't let go

they have let go

of sense

of wariness

to splash open faced to sunshine,

dogs, tamales, tubs of lemonade:

thick lemon slices that float in sugar ice.

"Zinnias" by Diane Kavanaugh-Black, copyright 2022, previously published at ofthessenceblog.com, used by permission of the author, all rights reserved.

The **Barnegat Poets'** received us with open arms. It was a great evening of reading, and luxurious bathing in the silver-blue waters of poetry, almost as refreshing as a dip in Pyramid Lake!

*****

Gwen, Maddy, Diane and I ended our make-shift retreat on Friday evening with a Zoom supper. We blessed our gathering and food by singing the PLC Blessing, and revisited our disappointment in missing the *in-person* 2022 PLC Women Writer's Retreat. When the evening's conversation and sharing was over, we agreed we'd been faithful to the spirit of PLC, had felt the magic, done some *"juicy writing,"* and made a refreshing *"lemonade"* of our *"real yellow lemon!"*

Lin Murphy Campfire Salutation to a Full Moon

Pyramid Lake September, 2022

I attended the **3rd Annual PLC Writerfest, September 11-16th, 2022.** I was able to get a Covid B-variant booster a week before I left for Paradox, and I was eager as ever to be at PLC again. I signed up for Tom Coash's playwriting class. Our pre-class assignment was to write a play, ten pages or less, and Tom provided a sample play with instructions to follow its format precisely.

Though I'd attended several of Sandi Dollinger's playwriting classes, and written a few scenes for plays, I'd never attempted to write a whole play, i.e. a drama in three acts, telling an *entire story* using only dialog.

"Well, it's a small class, Sue" Ellie O'Leary explained, *"and Tom understands he has beginners."*

I knew being with Tom would be a great experience. He's a well-respected, masterful playwright, and a beloved instructor in the Stonecoast MFA Creative Writing Program. I'd enjoyed the plays his students had written and performed at Writerfest 2019 and 2021, and *I wanted to think I could do this.*

I began writing by slapping some words of opening conversation onto a blank page, letting the tone of the first voice tell me who was talking and what might be happening. I did this a few times, but the characters and/or situations I created felt singularly uninteresting! *God Sue, your life's a bore!*

After this fiasco I went looking for inspiration on my

bookshelf, and pulled down a phenomenal, award winning piece of writing by Karen Hesse, a novel entitled *Out of the Dust*. This Young Adult novel, written in free-verse in the voice of Billy Jo, a 14 year old girl living in the bleak landscape of the dust bowl of Oklahoma, felt like something that could easily be adapted for the stage.

I was so excited about this possibility I wrote to Tom, told him about this book and my idea of adapting a portion of it for my assignment. Tom responded immediately, warned me about copyrights, and suggested that I search to see if a screen-play or play already existed. Sure enough, I discovered a movie was in the making.

A few days later, Tom wrote me again. He had read Hesse's book, and loved it. He told me it was true — this character's voice and this writing was made for the stage. He asked if I would mind if he used the book in our class to illustrate some points about monologue and narration.

Tom's interest in Hesse's book encouraged me. If I couldn't adapt Hesse's writing for the stage because it was copyrighted, and had already been scooped-up by screen writers, perhaps I could take comfort in the fact I had recognized a character and a piece of writing worthy of dramatization.

With time running out, I was struggling, when one

morning I awoke thinking about journalist Dorothy Thompson. I went to my bookshelf and pulled down every book I owned written by or about her. I'd gotten interested in Thompson back in 2016, when Donald Trump succeeded in getting himself elected President of the United States.

Trump's public biographical information included his father's involvement in the 1930's *America First* movement: a white nationalist, pro-Nazi, isolationist effort in which some members sported swastika's and attended rallies like the one held in New York's Madison Square Garden, in February 1939. This fact, and the creepy fact that a young Donald Trump had kept a book of Adolf Hitler's speeches in a locked drawer of his bedside table, made me want to read Thompson's pre-WWII journalistic efforts warning Americans about Hitler, and the threat of rising European and American fascism.

I knew Thompson had interviewed Adolph Hitler in August, 1932, and had been exiled from Germany after Hitler took power in 1934. I owned a rare copy of Thompson's book, *I Saw Hitler* (Farrar & Rinehart, NY 1932), and thought I could use it to create a fictional account of her meeting with him.

Here is the play I wrote for Tom's class.

Dorothy Thompson: *I Saw Hitler*

by Sue Cummings

Cast

Dorothy Thompson: Female, 40, American Journalist, the *"undisputed queen of the overseas press Corp,"* Head of the New York Post Berlin Bureau. Statuesque, handsome, a master of the dramatic entrance. Makes herself the center of attention, is aggressively gregarious and tireless in debate. For combined intellectual, physical, and emotional energy, she has no known equal, male or female.

"Happiness doesn't' matter — getting somewhere does...My dear, only fools and cows are happy. No intelligent human being is happy. If you suffer — well, what is that? Everyone suffers except horrible people who have no capacity. But one doesn't whine, and certainly one is never sorry for what has happened. Never...Courage and self-sufficiency are beautiful virtues."

Fluent in German, on assignment for Cosmopolitan Magazine in Munich, Germany to meet Adolph Hitler on August 17, 1932. She will publish a book entitled *I Saw Hitler*, and be exiled from Germany, in 1934. In 1939 she will be on the cover of Time Magazine, and be advisor to both Eleanor and Franklin Roosevelt. She will warn Americans about Hitler and fascism, both in Germany, Italy, and in the United States.

She is the 2nd wife of successful writer, Nobel Laureate, recluse and nasty drunk, Sinclair Lewis, and the mother of

Michael Lewis, age 2 ½.

'Red' Sinclair Lewis: Male, 47, a tall gangly red head, with a pocked marked face from teenage acne. In company he is either the center of attention and won't let anyone else speak, or is withdrawn and nasty. He is at the pinnacle of his career as an American Novelist; the first American to win the Nobel Prize for Literature (November, 1930). He is living with his 2 ½ year old son, Michael and a loyal Housekeeper/Nannie at Twin Farms, a 300 Acre Farm in Vermont with two houses.

He loves Dorothy, and when he's not drunk (which is rare) it is a fabulous match for both of them. He is at the height of his fame, is a keen critical observer of people, and a diligent writer, but he cannot control his drinking, and uses his acerbic, literate tongue as a lash. He will leave Dorothy in 1937, blaming her for the mediocrity of his writing, and divorce her in 1942. He has never had close personal friends, and prefers the life of a recluse.

German Waiter: Stefan

Telephone Operator: Female Voice

American Press Corp: 3 Male Voices (1, 2, 3)

SCENE 1

Synopsis

It's Tuesday, August 16th, 1932. Dorothy is in high spirits, drinking and dining with a few friends, mostly correspondents and their wives, in a downtown Munich Hotel. She is on assignment for Cosmopolitan Magazine, and tomorrow, August 17th, she will meet Adolph Hitler, an opportunity she has been seeking for 7 years. She will be exiled from Germany in 1934, a few days after Hitler assumes sole power over the German Parliament, becoming Chancellor and President (*"the leader"/ der Fuhrer*), following the decease of President von Hindenburg.

DOROTHY

You know what it's like, full of story that you can't get out. I was the only woman, and you know how men — well they don't take you too seriously. If I could scoop them all, I'd die happy!

(Sips her cocktail)

Once in Czechoslovakia I was stranded in a storm, had to wire my article to Vienna collect. The clerk at the telegraph office demanded payment in advance, so I wrote a note to Edvard Benes, the Czech foreign minister —"Beloved" I wrote. "will you bring pressure to bear to have the officials in this post office fired? I signed it "sweetie" and the clerk wired my article on the spot.

(Laughter)

STEFAN/WAITER

Excuse me Miss Thompson you have a transatlantic call. It's Mr. Lewis.

DOROTHY

Thank you Stefan. Excuse me everyone, please – go on without me.

(leaves the dining room with Stefan, who leads her to a small private room off the main foyer)

Good Evening Darling, can you hear me? Is everything alright. How is the writing? Tell me, is Michael happy!

RED

(with slurred speech throughout the scene)

Fine, fine, Michael's fine! He sits under my desk, chews my discards. He's a discerning editor. I miss you Dorothy ……. I want you home…. here with me. Have you met the bastard yet?

DOROTHY

I miss you too, Red. There's been a lot of fussiness connected with the meeting. His press attaché, I call him

Putzi, is an immense, high strung, incoherent clown.

I got a glimpse of the Little Man yesterday, racing through the lobby of the Kaiserhof surrounded by a lot of wavy-haired bugger boys--- pink cheeked mediocrities making a fetish of brotherhood, talking about woman's function in bearing SONS for the state.

His personal body-guard looks rather like Al Capone. He makes me a bit nervous. I'll let you know when I'm summoned. He's making me wait.

I'm here having dinner with Jimmy, Knickerbocker and his wife, Gunther and a few other guys on the beat. I'll call you after I file.

RED

Dorothy…. come home, I miss you. Ok, ok……………..ok, ok…………..……….yes I know, but I need you …….tell Jimmy he'd better keep you out of trouble!

SCENE 2

Synopsis

It's Thursday, August 18th, 1932, 2PM in Munich, and Dorothy is in her Munich Hotel Telephone Room, trying to reach Red. It is 8AM in Vermont, and Red is in his writing room, drinking his morning coffee.

(phone rings, sober Red picks up)

TELEPHONE OPERATOR

Hello is this Mr. Sinclair Lewis?

RED

Yes.

TELEPHONE OPERATOR

You have a transatlantic call from Miss Dorothy Thompson will you accept the charges?!!

RED

Yes, yes… I accept.

(scratchy phone noises)

Hello—Hello?… Dorothy? Dorothy can you hear me?

DOROTHY

Yes, RED! Can you hear me?.............. I met him.

RED

Tell me….tell me!

DOROTHY

He was late, of course. Kept me waiting in Hanfstaengel's room. Called an Italian journalist ahead of me.

I tell you Red, this man is contemplating power… already has a foreign policy: A German-English-Italian alliance to crush the power of France on the continent.

RED

Not surprised he kept you waiting. As for his aspirations, he told us in that rag of a book what he plans to do!

DOROTHY

I was expecting to meet the future dictator of Germany, but in less than fifty seconds I was sure I was not. This man is startling insignificant, Red!

He's a formless, faceless man…. his frame is cartilaginous. He's a caricature, inconsequent, ill poised…his movements are awkward, undignified…. un-martial. I'd say effeminate. Bet he holds his pinky finger in the air when he sips his tea!

RED

That figures!

DOROTHY

He rants… Red! speaks to me as if he were addressing a mob, and there's a hysterical note that creeps into his voice when he gets going.

And get this, when the conversation is the least bit

personal, he's the exact opposite. I'd say he's shy......
almost embarrassed, always seems to be searching for a
theme, something that might set him off again.

The scary part is... I see no trace of any inner conflict.
None. He speaks about Germany like a man in a trance.

On the subject of the constitution he was quite explicit.

"I'll get into power legally" he said. *"I'll abolish this parliament,
and afterward the Weimar constitution. I'll found an
authoritarian-state, from the lowest cell to the highest, everywhere
there will be responsibility! ... authority above... discipline and
obedience below!"*

He says *"When the German people are unified, secure in their
honor, France will respect us!" "We will arm! The child's spelling
book and the largest newspaper, all will be put in the service of our
mission! Our whining will be changed into a glowing prayer: God
bless our arms! Let the French march! Let us see whether African
niggers can conquer free Germany!"*

Red, he's a fascist, with a racialist, antisemitic philosophy,
teaching that Aryans and especially Nordics are created to
rule the earth — and he's mixed it all up with a muddled
socialism.

His mission, is the dissolution of the German Republic...
the establishment of a dictatorship, and the organization
of a new — Militant Germany.

He's gone to school on Mussolini. When he appears

between columns of cheering saluting crowds, he wears Mussolini's frown… saluting the crowds, exuding *decision, will-power, and dominance.* He says "crowds are like women —- you've got to treat them rough, they love it when you're strong!"

He's a *bono fide* demagogue Red, and he's got a vast audience. It's mostly an offended middle class mob he's exciting, and I tell you they're ready to do whatever he wants.

He's making them feel proud to be Germans again, riding the wave of twelve years of misrule for which the Allies, and the whole world are responsible.

And what a propagandist! He began with seven men, now there are seven million following him. He claims at the next election he'll control 15 million voters.

You can fight an idea with another idea, Red, and a better one, but better ideas have gone begging here. Nobody can stop him with argument. He appeals to invisible realities, to emotions, to faith rather than reason. Of course, he hates the press.

I judge his power by the effect he has on the masses. He told me that the function of speech-making is not the telling of truth. He lies, and doesn't blink an eye. He believes what he says.

If one is in debt, if one has not made a success of life — he tells the mob — *one still belongs to the German Race!* And

Germans are a superior Race. That is his message, Red! That is the whole of his message, that and revenge!

Patriotism, that's what he's selling, and hundreds of thousands of people, all over Germany, are meeting in monster rallies. They're buying it.

Two hundred thousand young men, all gymnasium trained bruisers in brown shirts, are his personal, private militia. They'll do anything for him. Anything!

Looking at this man, I saw a whole panorama of German faces, men whom this man thinks he will rule, and I thought " *Mr. Hitler you may get, in the next elections, the fifteen million votes you expect…but fifteen million Germans* CAN *be wrong!*

Scene 3

Synopsis

It's September, 1934. Dorothy has been exiled from Germany by personal order of Adolf Hitler, who has become both Chancellor and President of Germany, on August 2, 1934.

Dorothy is descending the gangplank of the *SS Leviathan* in NYC, waving to the crowd below, arriving to a heroines' welcome. Americans see her as the embodiment of the war against Fascism, not just in Germany, but also the growing, America First, domestic version.

Red is on the pier below, waiting to be reunited with Dorothy. He stands quietly aside, out of the lime light, while Dorothy is adored, and meets with the press. She is asked what America can expect from Germany.

This is the beginning of Dorothy's celebrity in America. In 1939 she will be on the cover of Time Magazine, and next to Eleanor Roosevelt she'll become the most influential woman in America.

Going forward, Red will make himself an outsider in the social circles of journalistic, political, cultural celebrity in which Dorothy will thrive. He will leave Dorothy in 1937, suffer a breakdown, and divorce her in 1942. Throughout he will blame Dorothy for the mediocrity of his writing. Except for his 1936 book, *It Can't Happen Here,* which describes the rise of a US dictator similar to Adolf Hitler, Lewis will never again receive literary acclaim.

Scene 3

(crowd noises, cheering, and calling out Dorothy! Dorothy! Dorothy descends the gangplank waving like Royalty. A crowd of reporters is waiting at the foot of the gangplank, ready to hear what she has to say.)

Press-Voice 1

Miss Thompson, Miss Thompson, can you tell us what we can expect from Hitler?

Dorothy

Boys, it's 'tyranny', 'murder', 'blackmail' and 'war' you can expect. These are the aims of his regime, and there's no turning back. Germany has already gone to war, and the rest of the world does not yet believe it.

I tell you the truth, the German people have not had Mr. Hitler thrust upon them, he recommended himself, and they bought him. They bought the pig of autocracy in a poke, because they did not know, or even ask exactly what form it was going to take.

It's an illusion, incurably cherished by the Anglo-Saxon mind that all peoples love liberty, and that political liberty and representative government are indivisible. Another illusion is that people are less aggressive than their rulers. I promise you, they are not!

We are witnessing a German aggression that has nothing to do with being German; the vast majority of ordinary mortals, are impatient in troubled times, and Hitler has come to power, simply because so called civilized, good people did not believe he could.

Press- Voice 2

Miss Thompson, Miss Thompson….. What's to be done about Hitler?

DOROTHY

The greatest enemy of Fascism is the people — I'm speaking here about private persons, individually or in aggregate, who insist on calling their souls their own. The enemy of Fascism is reason.

No people ever recognize their dictator in advance. No one ever stands for election on a platform of dictatorship. Hitler represents himself as the instrument for expressing the National will.

When our American dictator turns up you can depend on it, he'll stand for *everything* traditionally American. He'll be telling you he can make America Great Again!

Since the great American tradition is Freedom and Democracy you can bet our dictator, God help us! will be wrapped up in Red White and Blue, calling for more Freedom and more Democracy. He'll proclaim himself and his followers true patriots, and condemn anyone who is against him.

Americans have to face the reality that liberal democracy is the most demanding of all political faiths! It is a political philosophy which makes painful demands. It has a price.

Gentlemen, there really are such things in the world as morality, law, and conscience. These, once awake, are stronger than any ideology.

Press-Voice 3

Miss Thompson, Miss Thompson…..what are you going to do now?

Dorothy

Me, I want to live in a world in which we have such things as contentment, freedom, personal pride, opportunity for self-development, love, affection, and spiritual purpose. I want to live in a warm world, a kind world, a human world.

I want to be on good terms with myself and others. And whatever governmental system fails to assist these simple human desires is a ghastly failure, even if it produces more goods, greater wealth, more economic stability and more national power that has ever been produced or concentrated before.

(Dorothy moves off through the crowd as best she can, and finally sees Red, standing apart from the crowd, waiting for her. She falls into his arms. They kiss and hold one another. He is ready to take her home to Twin Farms.)

*****

I was thrilled, when in Tom's class I got to listen while my classmates enacted my play. My Women Writers' Retreat friend, Hazel Aranha made a terrific Dorothy Thompson! She really took hold of the role, and caught Dorothy's swagger and attitude.

After the reading, Tom asked me what I thought of my play. I answered, "*I think it's a bit preachy.*" Tom asked me to think about what an audience would be *seeing* on stage.

I got it right away. There was *no action.* Just two people having a long distance telephone conversation with one person doing most of the talking. As a stage drama my play didn't work, but I wasn't disheartened. I could hear Dorothy Thompson's voice in my writing, and I know for certain her life, her character, *would make great theater* and/or movie.

My intense re-reading of Dorothy's writing, and revisiting Peter Kurth's biography of Dorothy (*American Cassandra,* Little Brown and Company, 1990) to create my play for Tom's class, was an invaluable experience. It caused Dorothy to come alive for me: to become a living, flesh and blood breathing woman, with a body, a voice, a tone, motives, longings, flaws, personal and public history. It was an intimate experience. To date, my most valuable, exciting lesson in learning to write character.

Thank you Tom!

*****

It's December 2022, and I just learned that **Neil Bradt**, my very own 2015 *"superhero, greeter-in-chief"* has been appointed Interim Director of PLC in 2023. This may sound hokey, but I do believe Sr. Monica just winked at me!

Cornelius "Neil" Bradt and his wife Courtney

Pyramid Life Center

See you in July!

After-Words of Gratitude

Thank you to each and all my PLC Sisters who have supported me in years and years of retreats; especially **Sarah Sullivan, Beckie O'Neill, Debra Burger, Bonnie Harlan-Stankus, Carol Whitlow, Diane David Schneider, Hazel Aranha, Jane Eagles, Yvona Fast, Liza Apper, Lin Murphy, Nelle Stanton, Kay Patterson, Mary Baker, Ann Samson, Mary McCarthy, Pam Clements;** and more especially **Ellie O'Leary, Mary Bilderback, Kathy O'Brien, Cynthia Brackett -Vincent, Carolyn Mills, Gwen Marable, Maddy Spadola, Undine Giguere, Diane Kavanaugh-Black, and Mary Cuffe-Perez** *for their friendship, close reading, and suggestions for improving this memoir.*

Thank you to each and all my *LBI and Barnegat Writer* friends who have supported my poetry/writing habit over the years; especially **Margaret Hawke** (founder of the LBI Adult Writers Group), **Richard Morgan** (founder of the LBI Poets' Studio), **Norma Paul** and **Kathy Santangelo** (founders of the Barnegat Poet's Society) **Jim Curley** (Friends of the LBI Library), **Cindi Graham** (SCOSA Memoir) **Dottie LaMantia, Kim and Jim Trotto, Jeanne Harpster**: and more especially **Deborah Morales, Alise Versella, Aileen Reynolds, Nancy Kunz,** and **Jeanne Sutton** *for their friendship, writerly encouragement, and invaluable editorial assistance with this memoir.*

Thank you to each and all my friends, neighbors and family who have put up with my writing mania over the years; especially **James Fitz-Randolph, Elizabeth Kurz, Kenny Anderson, Bob Pritchard, Mike and Susie Cummings, Rick and Mary O'Meara, Jackie O'Meara, Cathy Pritchard, Dawn and John Kaltenbach, Lynn Denyers, Kim Smith,** and more especially **Margaret Hartwell, Gwenn Hotaling, Mei Stone, Arlene Marcoe and Woods Davis, Gary and Sue McElroy, Roberta Turner,** and **Nancy Gallagher** *for listening* to my endless PLC stories, *reading* early and late versions of the text of this memoir, and *enduring* my ever high enthusiasms.

Thank you to each and all the participants of my "Writing Down the Bones" Writing Practice Group. I wouldn't be celebrating the writing of this Memoir without you! I love you each and all, and as always, I'm ready to *Write ON!*

Pyramid Lake Stormy Morning Sunlight

September, 2022

Thank You Dominic!!

The Best Friend a Writer Could Ever Have

ABOUT THE AUTHOR

Sue Cummings is a 77 year old, retired research biologist and professor. She lives with her Border-Collie mutt Dominic, in the Edwin B. Forsythe National Wildlife Refuge, near Long Beach Island, New Jersey. In fulfilling a bucket list dream in 2012, she went Fly-Fishing on the *Youghiogheny River* in Western Pennsylvania, and came home *inexplicably* wanting to write poetry.

She joined her local LBI Adult Writers' Group, took a creative writing class for freshmen at Stockton University, and arrived at Pyramid Life Center (PLC) in 2015 to attend the Annual-July Women Writers' Retreat.

This memoir, is the story of her *"brief but spectacular"* PLC Writer's Life.

Sue is the host and coordinator of the LBI Poets' Studio, The Barnegat Poets' Society, and an on-line, weekly, *'Writing Down the Bones'* Writing Practice Group. She is a member of Philadelphia Great Books, and the Stockton University SCOSA Tour of Poetry.

She has several small publishing successes, and regularly contributes poetry to her local LBI Sandpaper.

Made in the USA
Middletown, DE
04 August 2024

58279951R00077